LITTLE CROSBY

Historic Village

Hugh Hollinghurst

Published by Mosslake Press for the Crosby Hall Educational Trust (CHET) a registered charity.

Printed in Liberation Serif by The Printing House, London

Front cover: Little Crosby village in the 1860s from a watercolour by Colonel Nicholas Blundell

Back cover: Little Crosby village today and Crosby Hall

The book may be used as a guide for a walk or tour of the village.

If you are walking or cycling the whole route, follow pages 6 to 27, pages 28 to 45 in reverse order, and pages 46 to 71. At the Ormskirk Lodge you can walk back by the footpath along the wall to the Liverpool Lodge and then return along the road to the Boundary Stone.

If you come by car, park in Oaklands Avenue by the Boundary Stone, follow pages 6 to 19 and repark at Delph Lane (page 30). You will see pages 20 to 27 on the way and can visit these on foot in reverse order after pages 28 to 44 if you wish. You will pass pages 46 to 71 on your way home.

Refreshments are available at the Courtyard Cafe in Delph Lane (page 30).

ACNOWLEDGEMENTS

To Mark Blundell for
    his encouragement, advice and multiple proofreading
    his generosity in making his writings available and giving me the benefit of the records of the Blundell family and his own personal knowledge
    the images on pages 6,7, 9, 11, 12, 13, 14, 15, 16, 17, 19, 20, 29, 33, 34, 53, 56, 57, 58, 59, 62, 63, 64, 65, 66 & 67

To Peter Owen for editing the book for print, for proofreading, and for his photos on pages 48, 49, 50 & 51

To the staff at the Local History section of the Sefton Library Service who helped me to use their archive

To the authors of the following:
    Margaret Blundell *A Lancashire Squire*
    Margaret Blundell *Francis Nicholas Blundell*
    Tom Gradwell *Life in Little Crosby*
    John Martin Robinson *Loyalty and Religion (Country Life, August 2015)*
    Frank Tyrer *Let's Walk to Little Crosby*
    Frank Tyrer *The Great Diurnal of Nicholas Blundell*
    Frank Tyrer *A Short History of St Mary's*

To Paul Barker/Country Life Picture Library for the photos on pages 26, 30, 31, 35, 39, 45, 46, 55, 56, 57, 59, 60, 61, 68, 70 and on the front and back cover

To Ordnance Survey and Paul Hollinghurst for the map opposite

To the following for their photos and images: Barb Connelly (page 55); Edmund Crighton (pages 25, 27 & 71); and the Crosby and District Historical Society (page 69)

Photos on pages 8, 22, 23, 24, 26, 33, 35, 36, 37, 38, 41, 42, 45, 52, 55, 56 and the back cover are by the author

To Vince Jones and Barry Partington who have helped me on the way

To my wife Joan as always for her understanding, support and patience.

The numbers on the map refer to the first of the two pages where the buildings at that location are described.

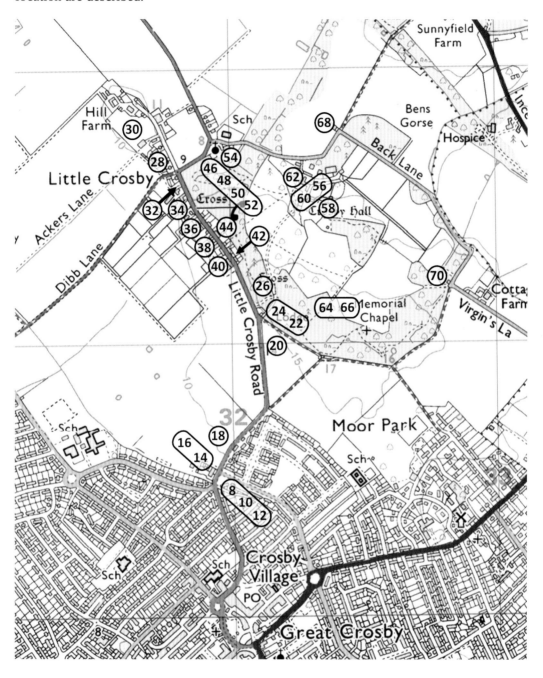

CONTENTS

Refer to the page numbers on the map on the preceding page for the locations of the buildings described.

[additional information in boxes including the story of the Blundells which can be followed in nine numbered sections] *Illustrations in italics*

Little Crosby, Domesday, and the Blundells

Little Crosby is built on rock, and out of the rock. Neolithic stones and axes have been unearthed here and the Vikings named it 'the place (-'by') of the Cross'. It is recorded as Crosebi in the Domesday Book of 1086. Before the Norman Conquest the manor was held by a Saxon Lord named Uctred, who also held other lands in South West Lancashire (marked * in the key to the map opposite). 'Crosseby Parva' (Little Crosby) is referred to in the 13th and 14th centuries and 'Little Crosby' from 1405.

The Blundells 1

The Blundells are descended from Osbert de Einulvesdel (Ainsdale), who held the nearby manor of Ainsdale in about 1160. In about 1189, his eldest son, Robert, additionally received a grant of the manor of Great Crosby from King John (then Count of Mortain), whom he served as a Royal Forester. His grandson, in turn (Sir) Robert, was the first of the family to use the surname Blundell. The neighbouring Blundells of Ince (Hinne) had the same name and there was probably some connection between the two families. Robert was also a tenant of some land in the manor of Little Crosby then held by the Molyneux family (p 27). One of his descendants, David, married Agnes sister of Sir John Molyneux. Sir John died in 1362 and the descendants of David and Agnes inherited the manor. The Blundells have remained there ever since.

Deed of grant of Great Crosby (Magna Crossebi) to Robert, the oldest document in the Blundell archive c1189

Small part of Burghley's map of 1590 showing Little Crosby (Blundale de crosbei). See The Blundells 2 *on page 9*

A map of places recorded in the Domesday Book. Near to Crosebi* are Sefton and Thornton. Walton is marked as the parish church for the area. Liverpool has yet to be born but is near the site of Esmedune (in Latin Esmeduna). Other recognisable places are Formby, Skelmersdale, Aughton*, Melling, Maghull*, Litherland, Kirkby*, Knowsley*, Roby*, Bootle, Kirkdale, Walton, (West) Derby, Wavertree, and Childwall.
*Lands held by Uctred in 1066

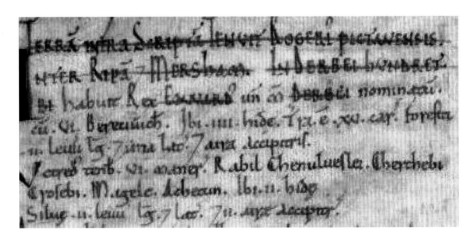

(Little) Crosby is at the start of the second line from the bottom of this extract from the Domesday Book. Great Crosby was a royal manor and therefore excluded from the Domesday Book.

Boundary Stone

A little two foot high triangular stone with no identification masks great importance, significance and history. It was originally inscribed with the names 'Great Crosby' and 'Little Crosby' to mark the boundary between the townships: a brook which has long since been culverted (p 12). However, the inscription was defaced to confuse potential invaders during the Second World War, and never restored. This boundary between the townships for hundreds of years ceased in 1932 when Great Crosby and Little Crosby merged to form one Urban District which later became part of the Borough of Sefton in 1974.

You are on the edge of the Liverpool conurbation. To the north can be seen open country and trees fringing the estate of Crosby Hall, home of the Blundell family for eight centuries. Beside its walls nestles the village of Little Crosby largely unchanged for over a century and most of it for much longer. To the south and east the stone marks the limit of the spread of the Liverpool conurbation that has engulfed Great Crosby during the same period. To the west as you walk forward to Little Crosby you can hear and see the trains running on the line between Liverpool and Southport. The railway, constructed in 1848, was built on land provided by the Blundells along the sea coast, thereby enabling the new residential development of Blundellsands in unproductive sandy land.

The Blundells 2: Richard and William the Recusant

During the late Middle Ages, the family prospered, but its decision to adhere to Catholicism after the Reformation created problems in the late 16th century. In 1590 Lord Burghley, Queen Elizabeth's Secretary of State, was trying to put down the Roman Catholic religion and a map was drawn up for him (p 6). On it he or his spies marked a cross against the families that were suspected of being Roman Catholic and needed watching, and 'Blundale de Crosbie' has a cross marked against him. The head of the family, Richard Blundell, died in Lancaster Castle on 19 March 1592, having been imprisoned there for the treasonous crime of harbouring a seminary priest. His son and heir William 'the Recusant' (that is, he refused to attend the Protestant church services) was also imprisoned at Lancaster and, later, London. He was pardoned at the accession of James I, although he was later heavily fined because of the Little Crosby riots (p 44). He took advantage of his freedom to rebuild Crosby Hall and establish the Harkirk burial ground (p 64). A reminder of the family on the front of Crosby Hall (p 56) has the initials **R**ichard **B**lundell, **A**nne **B**lundell his wife and **W**illiam **B**lundell his son.

Boundary Bridge

Until about 150 years ago the road from Great Crosby to Little Crosby was just a cart track and a plat or bridge made of stone slabs crossed a brook which marked the boundary. It was known as 'Ston Plat'.

In 1664 William Blundell, known as 'the Cavalier', Lord of the Manor of Little Crosby, threatened to sue Great Crosby for neglecting to keep the plat in repair. The plat had fallen in, blocked up the brook, and this caused flooding in his fields. He complained to Great Crosby but they ignored his complaints, until he threatened to take the matter to the Quarter Sessions, when Great Crosby immediately decided to act. An agreement was reached on the terms that Great Crosby should do the repairing, that William Blundell would not charge Great Crosby for any damage which had been done to his crops and fields, and that in future both townships would keep the bridge in good repair. The stone slabs to repair the plat were obtained from the Delph at Little Crosby (p 30) and recorded in the accounts:

> *Jun 21, 1665 - Received from John Ainsworth for stons, sold to the people of Great Crosby for a plat..8s 0d.*

> *October 11, 1665 For stons which were used by Little Crosby towards the repayer of one half of the Wheat hey ston plat................................8s 0d.*

Oaklands Avenue

Oaklands Avenue is named after the old name of the fields 'Oaklands' or 'Okelands'. These fields were so called as far back as 1275. Other names, for example Harkirk, can be traced back equally as far in history. They can tell us about the past, for example 'Townfield' (p 18), so it is helpful to have them preserved in road names and for road names to be preserved.

The Great Hodge Podge (opposite), a manuscript volume containing odds and ends of data from Elizabethan to Victorian days, was started by William the Recusant. This extract shows a list of army ranks and a doodle of a cavalier.

The Blundells 3: William 'the Cavalier'

William 'the Recusant' was succeeded in 1638 by his grandson, William 'the Cavalier', celebrated for the letters and notes he wrote over a period of 53 years. He served the King during the Civil War as a captain of dragoons, raising a troop of 100 men in 1642. As well as being lamed for life in a skirmish, he was imprisoned on several occasions. His lands were sequestered as a 'Papist and Delinquent', but later he was able to reacquire them with the help of Protestant friends. During the Commonwealth, William spent some time in exile on the Isle of Man and wrote a history of the island. A contemporary called him 'the great and learned Mr Blundell'. The Restoration of Charles II in 1660 brought a brief respite but trouble returned in the 1670s when hostility to Catholics grew ever more intensive. His Jesuit son Nicholas narrowly escaped with his life from the Popish Plot of 1678 and William himself had to escape to France. In 1690, he was imprisoned yet again for eight months as a suspected Jacobite. Another son was tried (and acquitted) in his place for treason in the 'Lancashire Plot' of 1694. William married Anne Haggerston of Haggerston in Northumberland when he was just 15 in 1635. Their marriage was long and productive with a large family of 10 surviving children. Five of his seven daughters became nuns who lived all their adult life in Flanders. Two of his sons were priests.

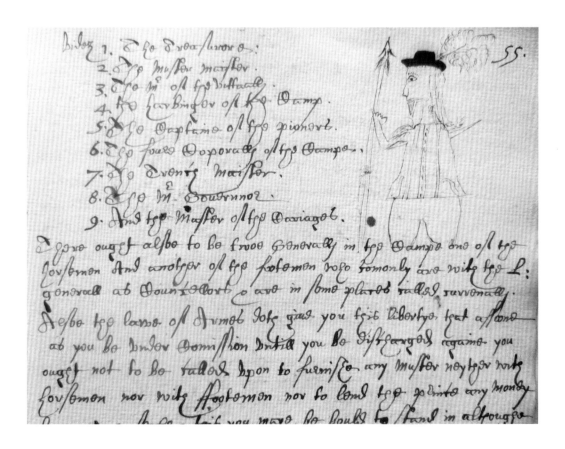

Boundary Brook

This Boundary Brook has, throughout the ages, been a constant source of dispute and trouble between the two townships (p 9). It was one of the many water courses used to drain off the water from the low lying land of the neighbourhood and therefore it was important to keep it clear so the water could run freely along it. Blockage of the water course led to flooding of the fields and destruction of vital crops, and such blockages frequently occurred, especially where the water course entered the sea. Gales and storms blew and washed the sand from the sandhills into it. When this happened the Manor Court of Great Crosby would complain to Little Crosby and suggest it was their job to scour it, and the Manor Court of Little Crosby would blame Great Crosby. Usually an agreement was reached that so many men from each township should be sent to scour the water course.

Nicholas Blundell often tells us in his diary that he went to see his men scouring this water course and frequently took them strong ale as refreshment. On one occasion he went to the boundary brook expecting to see men clearing it out, only to find that the men from Great Crosby were drinking in an ale house and not scouring the brook!

Left: Portrait of the Diarist

Right: Extract from Nicholas' diary 28 July 1709

The Blundells 4: Nicholas 'the Diarist'

In 1702, the manor of Little Crosby passed to the Cavalier's grandson Nicholas whose diary (or Great Diurnal) is well known to local historians. It extends from 1702 to 1728 with an entry for every day except one. He sketched the daily activities about the house, on the farm and in the garden and described the work, amusements and troubles of his tenants and labourers. He recorded his business and social engagements, his pastimes, the visits he and his family made, the comings and goings of friends and the medical treatments prescribed, observing anything of interest in normal daily activity as well as any unusual events.

Suspected of implication in the 1715 Jacobite rebellion, he escaped to Flanders for two years where he visited numerous relations and friends who were also there as refugees. On his return, Nicholas resumed his devotion to the estate, laying out formal gardens and renovating the house. His accounts (p 10) include payments for repainting the rooms, for new curtains for the windows in the gallery and two best rooms, and for repairing the beds in the Garden and Parlour chambers. He also developed a brickworks, making hundreds of thousands of bricks, for sale as well as for his own building on the estate. This included West Lane House (pp 54-5) which incorporated a chapel for the village, erected specially for the Catholic chaplain in 1719. Nicholas designed and supervised the building himself and celebrated its completion with 'a good bowl of Punsh' (no doubt made of contraband brandy, as he often mentions casks being hidden).

He married Frances, the daughter of Lord Langdale who was the grandson of the Royalist general Marmaduke Langdale. To their regret, Nicholas and Frances had no son. The diary contains many references to their two daughters, Mally and Fanny, who in their teens spent six years in Flanders for their education. Mally died aged 30, and Frances, who married Liverpool merchant Henry Pippard (Peppard), became Nicholas' heir (p 71).

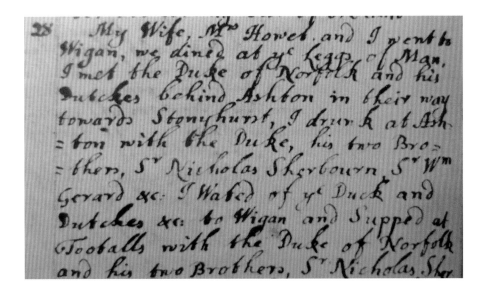

Boundary School

Opposite the Boundary Stone is Boundary Cottage (pp 8 & 16-17). It was built by William Blundell as a school in 1842 for the Roman Catholic children of Little Crosby, Great Crosby and the surrounding district. The opening in November 1843 was celebrated by a treat for the children, and the feast they were given by William Blundell's son, Nicholas, sounds very curious:

16th November 1843: New School opened, fair for it. Nicholas gave children: buns, negus and rice pudding, then made them run races, etc. Revds. Brown, Greenough and Shann there.

Frances and Catherine, the daughters of Squire William Blundell (see opposite) often assisted with the teaching in the school. As well as a school it was also a social centre where concerts and amateur plays were given, many of which were written by members of the Blundell family. It ceased to be a school in 1859, as new schools had been built for the education of Roman Catholic children: SS Peter and Paul's in Great Crosby, and St Mary's in the village of Little Crosby (p 54).

The plan for its conversion later into a house is shown below. Notice the entrance originally on the right hand side facing towards Little Crosby which was altered as on the plan to its present position with a frontage onto the road.

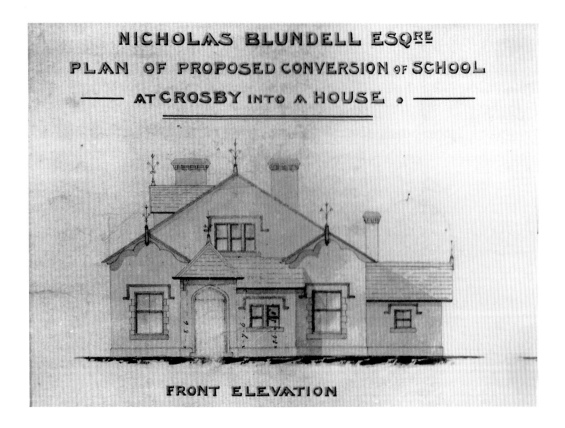

NICHOLAS BLUNDELL ESQRE
PLAN OF PROPOSED CONVERSION OF SCHOOL
AT CROSBY INTO A HOUSE.

FRONT ELEVATION

On ceasing to be a school, the building was occupied by the Yeomanry under the command of Squire Nicholas Blundell, who had succeeded his father William Blundell. He later became Colonel Nicholas Blundell. A newspaper cutting of January 1860 tells us of the event:

The services of the corps raised at Crosby on the 14th ultimo have been graciously accepted by her Majesty, and it now ranks as a company in the second division of the Volunteer Artillery forces of the County... Major Blundell has kindly placed a large room, formerly used as a school, at the disposal of the company for drill, which takes place every Monday and Thursday evening.

Right: William Blundell 'Fundator' (Founder)

The Blundells 5: William 'Fundator'

William Blundell, great grandson of Nicholas the Diarist, succeeded in 1795 and died in 1854. The Catholic Emancipation Act of 1829 allowed him to participate in public life and he served as one the first post-Reformation Catholic High Sheriffs of Lancashire in 1837. Catholic churches were now legal and William built a new church, St Mary's, in the village (pp 46-51). It is for this reason that he is called 'Fundator' (Latin for Founder).

In 1798 when William was just twelve years old his guardians bought the Manor of Great Crosby for him. He married Catherine Stanley, of the Stanley family of Hooton, and their arms (three stag heads) appear on the face of the Presbytery which was formed from West Lane House (pp 54-55).

As chairman of the Liverpool, Crosby and Southport Railway he was responsible for the foundation of Blundellsands (p 9). Helped by a booming agricultural economy, he and Catherine had the resources to create the library at Crosby Hall (pp 60-61), as well as the present garden (pp 58-59) and the walled park (p 22). Besides Boundary Cottage, William was responsible for a host of estate buildings: the lodges (pp 22 & 70) and the Bailiff's House in Virgins Lane (p 70), which were all designed by Lugar (p 23).

Boundary Cottage

In 1867 the Boundary School was transformed into a dwelling house 'to be known in the future as Boundary Cottage' (p 14). After its conversion into a cottage, it was occupied by the Volunteers. There used to be four muzzle loading cannons overlooking the boundary brook with a stack of cannons each weighing 32 lb., ready at hand, no doubt, in case of trouble and invasion from Great Crosby!

The Volunteers

A villager who was present at the time related:

There is one particular thing I can remember and it was the Crosby Company taking part in the great Review that was held in Knowsley Park, the seat of the Earl of Derby, in the year 1860. The reason why it is so well remembered is on account of the Company being at St. Mary's Church, Little Crosby, on the Sunday before the Review took place. On that same Sunday Old Jim Kaye, coming out of the Church (found) not much room for him with his crutches as he was only able to get about by the aid of crutches. He roared for them to move and get out of his way, as they were only Goddam buttermilk soldiers. I heard him say the words and that he could beat the lot of them himself, which caused a great laugh and (cries of) 'Well done, Jimmy, yore game yet!' 'Aye, and if you don't shift (continued Jim) I shall knock some of ye to d--- rags wi' my stick or crutch.'

Further alterations were made to the building in 1887 and 1888 when Colonel Nicholas Blundell's eldest son, William Joseph, began to live there. With the death of his father in 1894, William Joseph Blundell took up residence at Crosby Hall, and the cottage was first rented out and later sold. It is still in use as a dwelling house (p 8).

(left) Colonel Nicholas Blundell

The Blundells 6: Nicholas 'the Colonel' and William

Nicholas, son of William Blundell 'Fundator', and, in 1854, successor, became a Justice of the Peace and Deputy Lieutenant of Lancashire like his father. He was a Major in the Duke of Lancaster's Own Rifle Militia and appointed Lieutenant-Colonel Commandant in 1872.

He greatly enlarged Crosby Hall in 1867 by rebuilding the kitchen wing with a tower and adding a decorated porch (below). When his son and heir, William, came of age in 1872 he spared no expense to celebrate the occasion, even adding a magnificent ballroom to the house (see also pp 26, 49-50).

To recover the finances, the family migrated to Brussels, leaving William to lead an extravagant life style alone which he continued after his father's death in 1894. William's marriage had been annulled in 1888 and he died in 1909 without leaving an heir, although he claimed to have adopted a son. He was succeeded by his nephew Francis Nicholas (pp 32-33).

The Victorian additions were removed in 1954, when the house was restored to its original dimensions by Brian and Hester Whitlock Blundell, the parents of the present owner, Mark Blundell (pp 42 & 62).

William Blundell, chauffeur and dog

Marling

Just beyond Boundary Cottage towards Little Crosby are the playing fields of St Mary's College, Crosby. This was formerly the Townfield (or one of the townfields) of Little Crosby, a field over which the Lord of the Manor had no jurisdiction. It belonged to the peasants who farmed their own strips of land in this field. Later, strips were joined together to form fields.

In the middle of this field, until the early 1960s, was what appeared to be a pond with rushes growing round the edge: the remains of a Marl Pit dug out in 1677. Marl is a kind of limey clay that breaks up very easily, and was highly valued as a fertilizer for its property of improving light sandy soils in particular. 'Marling' (extracting it from the soil) was one of the important agricultural operations in Little Crosby, and all the community regarded marl getting as a great event. From early times portions of the land were marled in rotation every twenty years. In the 'Great Hodge Podge' at Crosby Hall (p 11) there is a record of the marling carried out by five generations of Squires during 150 years. Marlers went in groups from one estate to another, contracting with the landowner to bore for the clay, dig it out, and spread it in the agreed portion on the selected land. The lord of the manor would notify some of his tenants that he required them and their horses and carts for marling. This was one of the boon duties the tenants had to perform as part of their rent for the lord of the manor. First the top sods were taken off and then the marl was dug out, loaded into carts and taken to the field it was intended to marl. There it was spread out by others of the tenants and labourers. From this particular pit about 8,000 cartloads were dug out and used to marl two fields which at the present time are part of the hall grounds. There are records of over 20,000 loads in Little Crosby and over twice that amount elsewhere. The workers were given free beer and meat in addition to their pay. The cost was well worthwhile in the greater yield of crops from the marled field.

One curious custom in connection with marling was that of 'shouting'. Nicholas Blundell in his Diary (1702-1728) frequently tells us that when he took friends to see the marlers at work he made the marlers 'to shout', and for this entertainment the visitors gave the marlers ale or 2s 6d towards the cost of the festivities. They were 'shouting' for their ale (the term survives in Australian slang!).

The marl pit often created a pond or mere as at CHET (pp 62-63) shown above right with children rafting.

Flowering of the Marl Pit

(from Nicholas Blundell's Diary; his idiosyncratic and inconsistent spelling has been retained in this transcription and others.)

July 8 1712: I was very busy in the after Noone making Kaps, &c: for my Marlers & Dansers, severall of Great Crosby lasses helped me. The young Women of this Towne, Morehouses* and Great Crosby dressed the Garlands in my Barne for Flowering of my Marl pit. I tought my 8 Sword Dancers their Dance, they had musick and danced it in my Barn.

July 9 1712: I was extremely busy all Morning making some things to adorn my Marlers Heads. My Marl-pit which was made in the Great Morehey out of which I marled the Picke & Little Morehoy was flowered very much to the Satisfaction of the Spectators, there was present Ailes Tickley, Mrs Molyneux**…&c…they supped here, all the 14 Marlers had a Particular Dress upon their Heads and Carried each of them a Musket or Gun. The six garlands &c: were carried by young Women in Prosestion, the 8 Sword Dancers, &c: went along with them to the Marl-pit where they Dansed, the Musick was Gerard Holsold and his Son and Richard Tatlock. At night they Danced in the barn. Thomas Lathord of Leverpoole brought me to the Marl pit a Dogg Coller against my Bull Bate as is to be in the Pit.

The celebrations went on for several days with dancing in the Hall and in the Barn to the music of pipes and fiddles, and in the light of candles and rushes, while the home brewed brown ale provided flowed freely.

*   'Morehouses' is Hightown. The barn is now part of CHET (pp 62-63).
**   Alice Tickley and Mrs Molyneux of the Grange are given prominent mention
      again (p 28).

Mill and Meadow

On the right going in to Little Crosby between the last houses of the housing estate and the gates of Crosby Hall is a triangular shaped field called Mill Meadow, suggesting that Little Crosby Mill was somewhere near it. This was built before 1275 and pulled down in 1813 when the one in Moor Lane was built to take its place. Its site was 50 yards from the Liverpool Lodge entrance inside the wall that encloses the Crosby Hall grounds, but all that remains is a slightly raised circular mound and a few broken bricks now buried under a tangle of bramble and bracken. The mill was essential for everyone's daily bread and useful for the tenants who had their corn ground and for the lord of the manor as a source of income. For many centuries this was taken as a fraction of the ground corn and in the 18th century the tenants had to pay to be excused from grinding at the mill. It was also useful in the times of recusancy as a lookout post for agents sent to search the Hall. It was a great disaster when the mill, with its six sails instead of the usual four, was destroyed in 1710 and every effort was made to reopen it two months later. The village tailor (p 36) was employed to remake the sails as he did each year (usually in June when it was not busy) besides running repairs.

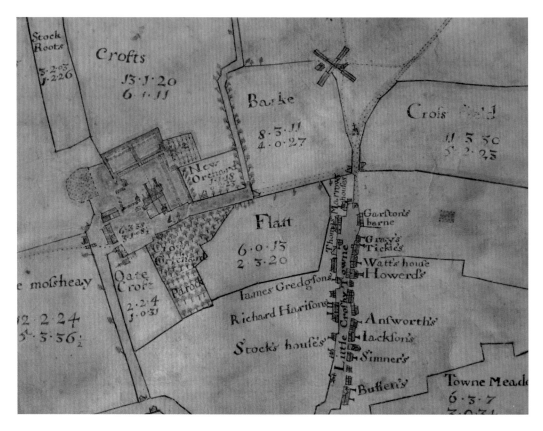

Hawley's 1702 map (orientated with south to the top). The windmill is clearly marked (top right) with the Wayside Cross just below it (p 26). Crosby Hall is centre left. The church is now at the junction of the roads on the bottom left. There is a detail of the village on page 29.

The Blundells 7: John and Henry the Rogues

John Blundell (c1330-1374) was the son of David and Agnes Blundell (p 6). He was a wild youth. He and his brother Henry are described in the reports of the Assizes for 1350 as 'common malefactors' when they were accused of taking 'with force of arms' five oxen valued at eight shillings from John de Gosfordsiche in Little Crosby 'on Wednesday next after the Assumption of the Blessed Virgin Mary contrary to the King's peace'. The two brothers were also accused of stealing corn and animals from the dowry land of their stepmother. John was an orphaned minor and so Sir John Molyneux, as his feudal overlord, had the right to choose his bride, and to fine him if he refused to follow his choice. But at the Assizes in July 1351, Sir John complained that, although he had often offered his ward John suitable marriage, he had rejected the offer. Not only did John reject Sir John's marriage proposals, but he was excessively keen to seize hold of his inheritance. Ten years later, at the Assizes of 1361, when Sir John was still living, he laid a series of claims to areas of land in Little Crosby to which he believed he was or would be entitled. No fewer than eight claims were lodged, for areas of one to five acres, from different neighbours.

John had no living son when he died in about 1374 so the lordship of Little Crosby passed to his brother Henry who held it for over thirty years. Henry continued to frequent the law courts. In 1384 a suit was lodged against him by John of Gaunt, the Duke of Lancaster and holder of the royal manor of Great Crosby. The presentment, by twelve jurors, claimed that Henry pastured 200 cows, 12 bullocks and 300 sheep on the Duke's grass in Great Crosby, permitted his men to fish in the Duke's fisheries of the Mersey, and threatened the Duke's reeve (agent). But by 1387 Henry seems to have turned over a new leaf, because in that year a licence was granted to him by the Bishop of Liverpool (for a suitable fee, no doubt) to allow him to have an oratory in Little Crosby, thereby giving Henry an opportunity to atone for his sins.

Later there was another Henry Blundell (1517-1556). His grandson tells us that he was a very bad husband. He was a great drinker and had leased all the demesne lands but one close (small field) which he reserved for the horse that carried him daily to the Ale house. By contrast, however, Nicholas Blundell (1447-1523), who was hounded by Dame Anne Molyneux (p 27), had a happy marriage for sixty years in which it is recorded they 'never cold find fote noder with oder' (never could find fault with each other).

Liverpool Lodge

On the bend of the road before reaching the village you come to the Liverpool Lodge entrance to Crosby Hall. This grand gateway was built by William Blundell 'Fundator' (p 15) as part of his project to create a fashionable park of woodland and pasture. He relocated the windmill (p 20) to Moor Lane where it still stands, started planting trees and built a stone surrounding wall. It was built from the gate to the first house in the village in 1813. Between 1817 and 1819 it was continued right round to the stables by the Hall, while between 1821 and 1828 the Liverpool Lodge, just the other side of the gate, the Ormskirk Lodge in Virgins Lane, and the wall between them were built. By 1835 the Hall grounds were completely encircled by the wall which is about three miles long. The stone was obtained from the Delph or quarry in the Village (p 30).

Left: lodge gateway. The gates date from 2010. A close up of one of the lions appears on page 24.

Left: Liverpool Lodge

Robert Lugar

Although born in Colchester, England, Lugar (1773-1855) carried out much of his most important work in Scotland and Wales, where he was employed by several leading industrialists to design grand houses such as Balloch Castle, Cyfarthfa Castle, the Rectory in Yaxham, Norfolk, now known as Yaxham House, its mirror image at Ffrwdgrech House in Brecon and Bardon Hall in Leicestershire. He was a versatile architect, designing the Liverpool Lodge in Italianate style, the cottage ornée Ormskirk Lodge (p 70) with frilly bargeboards and lattice windows, the Bailiff's House in Virgins Lane (p 70) and Boundary Cottage (pp 8 & 14-17). He published a handbook of designs for such buildings called 'Country Gentleman's Architect' and 'Hints for Dwellings' copies of which are in the library at Crosby Hall. The range of designs extended from a labourer's cottage and dog kennel to farm houses, villas and castellated mansions (see below).

Left: a typical design by Lugar for a lodge (not used on the Crosby estate)

Blundell Crest and Shield

On the Liverpool Lodge gate posts (below and page 22) is the crest of the Blundell family: half a lion rampant, holding in its paws a cross tau fitchée, that is a cross pointed at the lower end with the top arm of the cross omitted. The tau is an old form of representing the cross of Calvary. A friar would carry such a cross on his travels and, when he came to some inhabited spot, would thrust the pointed end into the ground and there begin to preach.

The lion on the other side of the gate lost the tip of its tail in a war-time accident (below).

The Blundell crest and shield appear on a house in the village with the initials of Francis Nicholas Blundell (pp 32-33)

The arms of the family, ten silver billets (representing logs of wood) are on a black shield. We know Robert Blundell (p 6) was knighted sometime after 1254 and that he used this shield. The source of this motif has been debated. It has a strong resemblance to the shield of the de Boulers (Robert's mother-in-law), recorded c1285, which also has billets, though the latter has in addition a 'Bend Argent', or silver band, diagonally across it. It may very well be that this was the source of the Blundell shield. The Blundell family of Ince later adopted the 'Ten Billets', but not until 1613, and with a difference. Before that date, they had a different shield altogether. Why they adopted their neighbours' shield in this way is a mystery.

Blundell Coat of Arms

Shield of Baldwin de Boulers

Inscription on the wall of Crosby Hall with exaggerated tau cross

Sefton Church Hatchment: the Blundell arms impale those of Langdale of Holme (Nicholas the Diarist married Frances Langdale)

Wayside Cross

As you go along the road from Great Crosby towards Little Crosby, 100 yards further on from the Liverpool Lodge is a cross in the wall. This is a reminder of the old Wayside Cross which stood by the old road. The cross still stands but has been hidden by the building of the wall. It was one of the funeral or wayside Crosses which can be traced

from Hightown through Little Crosby to Sefton Church. At each Cross the bearers of their deceased friend would put down the body and rest awhile and say a prayer before they continued their journey to Sefton Church. Squire Nicholas Blundell's watercolour paints a beautiful picture of the rugged cross. Most of the head has gone but the pedestal stands on two steps, very much worn, no doubt, by various celebrations round the Cross in ancient days and by the footsteps of worshippers in their religious devotions. One ancient custom of the district was the Flowering of the Cross when children and adults brought garlands of flowers to decorate the Cross. Possibly a religious ceremony, it was also an occasion for meeting friends.

The Wayside Cross

This is the first of a number of water-colours painted by Colonel Nicholas Blundell that are illustrated in the book. They were painted in the 1860s and the originals are in Crosby Hall.

The Molyneux Family and the Blundells 8

The Molyneux family of Sefton were lords of the manor of Little Crosby before the Blundells. The Molyneux, as their French name indicates, were granted lordship by William the Conqueror or one of his barons. Early in the 13th century Adam Molyneux gave his second son Roger the manor of Little Crosby. Sir Robert Blundell was a free tenant of some land there. Later the manor of Little Crosby passed into the Blundell family through the marriage of Agnes Molyneux with David Blundell (p 6). The Blundells still paid a nominal rent of 4d a year to the superior lords of Sefton. In the early 16th century, Dame Anne Molyneux, who for some reason bore a grudge against Nicholas Blundell, forcibly evicted him from Crosby Hall, claiming it was her rightful property. Nicholas went to the courts, including the Star Chamber. It was only after Nicholas died in 1523 that the case was finally settled in favour of the Blundells and their rights as the lords of the manor of Little Crosby were fully recognised. However, Nicholas's son Henry fought on the same side as Sir William Molyneux at the battle of Flodden (1518). Henry was killed but William survived to be buried in the Molyneux church of Sefton and there is a picture in brass on the floor of the choir showing him in the armour he probably wore at Flodden (below).

According to William the Cavalier, Henry *'left or had (as I have heard my Grand-father Wm. Blundell say) 24 children, by two wives, wch marying for the most part to poore Neighbours raysed up a beggarly kindred to the Family.'* Henry was only married for 24 years in all so a total of 24 seems unlikely, though not absolutely impossible.

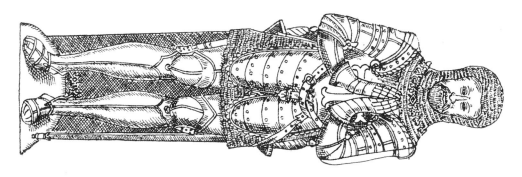

Brass of William Molyneux in Sefton Church

Hawley's Map of 1702

The map is orientated with south to the top and is ideal for using if you are starting from the Courtyard Cafe and Four Lane Ends to walk through the village. Note that the village is referred to as a 'Towne' as was customary then. Buildings named on the map are in **bold**. Some of the family names are mentioned in the diary of Nicholas Blundell as shown below but cannot be assigned to the houses with certainty. In order, starting from Four Lane Ends (bottom right) they are :

Answorth's: William Ainsworth was a tenant of Nicholas and lodged with him, being paid £1 a quarter as steward (in Nicholas' list, the priest was paid £2 and the miller most of all £2 5s). He played a key role in marling (pp 18-19).

Richard Harison's: He was the pinner (in charge of the pinfold, p 31), tenant and servant of Nicholas, and also stood as umpire and witness for him. Nicholas visited him with his wife to eat Christmas fare (on 16th January!). When Richard died, his widow, Ellen, went on walks with Nicholas' wife and served in the Hall, taking over from her daughter in law Betty (nee Farer, p 43). Betty had served as chamber maid and dairy maid for a year at 10s a quarter until she had to resign to look after her child. Ellen frequently went over to help her and Nicholas' wife had 'strong debate' with her about her daughter-in-law. Once she was blown over by the wind and badly bruised. One of the longest entries in Nicholas' diary concerns a supernatural vision that Ellen had at Crosby Hall on Christmas Day 1717. She served the poor on behalf of Nicholas who witnessed to her will and she was buried at Sefton Church.

The **barn**, just beyond **James Gredgson**'s on the left, still stretches along the road, adjoining Heatherlea Farm house.

Howerd's: see page 38.

Tickle's: John Tickle (or Tickley) was a yeoman farmer and overseer of the poor account that had to be read in Sefton Church. He was intimate enough with Nicholas to tell him of 'his secret and greatest trouble'. They went coursing together on numerous occasions and their financial affairs were complicated and interrelated. John owed a £20 fine to Nicholas who paid to John a tax imposed on Roman Catholics. Meanwhile, John had to borrow £30 from the miller and Nicholas had to make up a misunderstanding over arrears in rent owed to him by John and his son Richard, also a yeoman farmer. Father and son seem to have been quarrelsome. Richard was put into the stocks after a fight whilst drunk and Nicholas had to adjust a quarrel in which John was involved. However, Richard's wife Alice was one of the first to be invited to Crosby Hall with Mrs Molyneux of the Grange for Nicholas to present his new wife and give them supper (see also p 19).

Thomas Marrow's house: see page 18.

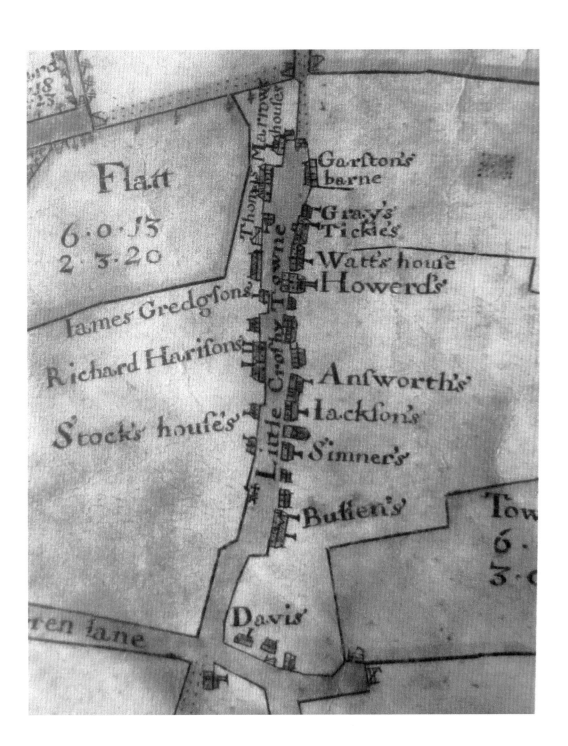

Flatt

6 · 0 · 13
2 · 3 · 20

Iames Gredgsons

Richard Harisons

Stock's houfe's

Thos: Marton's houfes

Little Crofby Towne

Garston's barne

Gray's Tickie's

Watt's houfe

Howerd's

Anfworth's

Iackfon's

Sinner's

Butlen's

Tow
6 ·
3 ·

Davis

ren lane

page 29

The Delph

The lane leading to the site of the Delph or quarry leads off Delph Lane opposite the Courtyard Cafe. The Delph appears to have been first used in the early 1600s. No doubt the stone for Crosby Hall came from here. In the 1660s a great deal of stone was quarried from the Delph by William Blundell the Cavalier to make alterations and additions to Crosby Hall (p 56) and also to build the 17th century cottages in the Village (pp 36-37). In this period of great activity the stone getter was paid 7d a day, and others from the Village who assisted him 6d a day.

In 1846 stone from this Delph was used in building Boundary Cottage (pp 14 & 16), St Mary's Church, Little Crosby (p 46), and also, at a later date, St Joseph's Catholic Church, Blundellsands, as well as the memorial to Francis Nicholas Blundell (p 33). The last stone was taken from it in 1890 for building purposes, apart from that for the memorial. It was then known as the Crane Pit because a crane was used to lift the stone. It fell into disuse because of the difficulty in pumping water out which flooded into it, and in 1953 it was filled in.

Below: looking south towards the village from the Delph. An outcrop of the quarry can be seen on the right and the Courtyard Café now occupies the buildings on the left.

The Pinfold and Stocks

The old Pound or Pinfold of the Village was situated where Hill Farm is at the end of this short lane. Managed by the Pinner (p 28) it was here that stray cattle were kept until claimed by their owner, who had to pay a fine to the Constable. Frequently we read in old Court Rolls of villagers being fined by the Manor Court for breaking into the Pinfold and taking out their impounded cattle without paying the Constable. It was even broken into by men from Great Crosby and used by the Morehouse (Hightown) pinners. In 1711 some cows were put into one of Nicholas the Diarist's fields that had a bull in it without his permission in the hope that they would be serviced and Nicholas impounded them.

The Pinfold has now gone, as also have the Stocks where, in May 1724, William Pinington and Richard Tickley were punished for fighting (p 28), as also was John Radcliff in February 1727 for 'Night Walking, Breaking Windows and forcing open Ailes [Alice] Davys Doar'.

Nicholas observed and recorded a form of public shaming which he called 'riding'. This was inflicted on a woman who had beaten her husband (more often it was the other way round). A cart was drawn through the village in which were two men one of them dressed as a woman and holding a basting ladle in his hand. At each place they stopped, the 'woman' belaboured the culprit with it and they shouted at each other. A procession of men and boys followed blowing horns in a riotous display.

Below: Quarry Cottage, now named Hill Cottage

Four Lane Ends and Memorial

The cross roads at the north end of the village used to be known as Four Lane Ends. To the west is Dibb Lane which leads to Sniggery Wood (where eels – snigs – were to be found) and Hall Road; to the east is the road to the Church and the 'Back Lane' to the Hall.

Notice that the roadway is lower than the field on the left and the churchyard on the right. Before 1845 the roads were muddy cart tracks. When William Blundell built the Church in 1845-6 he decided not only to improve the road, but also to lower its level at this point (known as the 'Hill'). He did this to make the Church look taller and more impressive. This was a tremendous task in days when there were no bulldozers and mechanical diggers, for it involved the removal of thousands of tons of soil for a distance of about two hundred yards from the Well Cross to the Four Lane Ends and from there to the Presbytery just beyond the Church.

On Easter Monday 1713 Four Lane Ends was the scene of a great Cockfighting event which attracted the gentry and tenants from a wide area around. Indeed, it seems to have been a favourite spot for such sport.

On the front of the two red brick houses built in 1910 at this corner to replace the old thatched cottages are the arms and crest of the Blundells of Crosby and the initials of Francis Nicholas Blundell who was then the Squire (p 24).

The Blundells 9: Francis Nicholas

It was not surprising that the villagers put up a memorial to Francis. On inheriting a neglected estate in 1909 (p 17) his first concern was for his tenants and he visited every cottage and farmhouse to assess their difficult situation. He had ten cottages built by local workmen (see opposite). He raised his workers' wages but kept their rent at the same level. Those in special need were helped with medical treatment and suitable clothing. He organised district farming federations that would create insurance against accidents and devoted himself to developing agriculture in the area (p 63). He was on the Lancashire County Council for 24 years and, after distinguished war service, was a Member of Parliament for seven years and chairman of the Catholic Education Council of England and Wales for nine years until his death. He was largely responsible for the passing of a bill to repeal the penalties that still applied to Roman Catholics. He presented Sniggery Wood to the town of Crosby. When Crosby was to become a Municipal Borough, he was chosen to be the first 'Charter' mayor but died in 1936 before he could take up office.

Across the road is the memorial erected by the villagers to the memory of 'Francis Nicholas Blundell, Esquire, who died on October 28th 1936' (below left). Francis Nicholas Blundell (below right) was devoted to the welfare of the villagers of Little Crosby and they chose this as their way of expressing their thoughts of him.

Well Cross

On the opposite side of the road to the Memorial is an old cross standing on a large sandstone base known as the Well Cross. It is near to the land which, as Hawley's map of Little Crosby shows, was once the 'Towne Meadow' or Green (p 20).

A Manor Court Roll of February 1616 refers to the provision of a pump '*in the newe well at the lower end of the Towne before Michaelmas next*'. The charge for putting in the pump was to be levied on the six people who lived nearest to the well and they were to have free use of it, while any others of the town who felt disposed to contribute were also allowed free use of it (others had to pay for any water they drew). In 1622 they were ordered to repair the covering over the Town Well and make a door to it '*Anyone refusing to do so would not be allowed to get water and would be fined 6s. 8d*'. It is interesting to note that half the fine would go towards the repair of the well and the other half to the lord of the manor!

When the cross was set over the well is not known. On Hawley's map of 1702 there is a cross shown on the other side of the road (p 20). Nicholas Blundell mentions in his Diary that on 23rd August 1710 a new Stone Cross was set up unknown to him in the Town by William Gray, the overseer of the highways (but not the cross which is there now). There would appear to have been some kind of dispute between the lord of the manor and William Gray, who seems to have been a trouble maker. In 1714 he was fined 2s 6d for '*Spoyleing and making unserviceable the water in the Town-well of Little Crosby to the rest of the neighbourhood*'. He also acted as smith (p 40). On the shaft of the cross appear the date 1758 and the initials I M or J M. To whom these refer is not known. The well supplied water to the village until the 1870s when the construction of a main sewer caused it to run dry. Note that someone is drawing water in Nicholas Blundell's painting opposite.

Some of the stones of the pedestal are well worn, but others are more recent. On some of the stones are glacial scratches, and this is an indication that the stones came from the Little Crosby Delph. Before the Delph or quarry was filled in it was possible to see in the rock there scratches made by the glaciers as they moved over it in the last Ice Age.

Mere Stones

Nearby is a garden of mere stones (boundary stones) with an informative map and tablet of information organised by the late Bob Wright (including the position of the Neolithic finds, p 6). Are these the mere stones which used to mark the boundary between Little and Great Crosby?

Henry Blundell (c1385-1457) is recorded as being involved in a dispute with the tenants of the Duke of Lancaster over the common boundary between the manors of Little and Great Crosby. Henry rode with an arbitrator and 16 tenants to survey the disputed area, setting up the meres then and there, after which, as in the Ince dispute (pp 68-9), a ditch was dug along the boundary. Later, in 1719, disputes were settled by juries from the two townships who met on the sea shore and amicably staked out fishing boundaries (see also p 12).

17th Century Cottages

In the middle of the village is a group of 17th Century cottages, one of which has a date stone, 1669, over the door and the initials I E which are a puzzle. This is the cottage named for John Ainsworth on Hawley's map (p 29). 'I' could stand for John (Iohannes in Latin) with E an earlier spelling 'Einsworth'.

The cottages, constructed of stone from the Delph in the Village, have altered little since they were built. The three white cottages on the opposite side of the road (named for Richard Harrison on Hawley's map) are constructed with a cruck or A-frame. The right hand one is said to be the Tailor's Cottage and for centuries the home of the village tailors. The stone ledging near the base of the cottage under one of the windows is very much worn and it is said that this may have been caused by the village children as they stretched up to see the tailor at work.

The framing of the date stone over the door has the same motif as the Boundary Cottage (p 14).

A Tailor's Job

A tailor's job was important and could be extremely varied and busy. Thomas Marrow, tailor, appears on the map of 1702 as living in the village (pp 28-29). He had to renew the sails of the windmill once a year and whenever there was storm damage (p 20). Thomas also worked a smallholding, his moss was used for turf delving and Nicholas Blundell the Diarist paid him land tax. All this involved Thomas in settling grievances associated with his land in regular settling of accounts and rent, and corn contribution to the lord of the manor, but he also had to have a difference settled between him and Nicholas in the presence of witnesses. Besides making Nicholas a new suit of clothes (trimmed with black) he was also called upon to do odd jobs at the Hall (like shaving behind Nicholas's ears and putting blistering plasters on!). Thomas left Nicholas' service on 1st January 1711 and shortly afterwards 'stated' accounts with him and paid his bill off.

John Answorth's House

Tailor's Cottages: Richard Harison's

The Priest's House

Towards the southern end of the village is a low white cottage with a stone slab roof and dormer window known as Ned Howerd's Cottage or the Priest's House. William Blundell the Cavalier (p 11) kept a record of his transactions with his tenants. In these 'Tenants Books' there is a note written in 1665 which states that because of the long and faithful service of John Howerd and Edward Denton, John's uncle, William Blundell, willed his heirs to show particular favour to the children of John Howerd. Nicholas Blundell the Diarist faithfully carried out this instruction and John's son, Ned Howerd, became a privileged tenant of this cottage and Nicholas' friend. The cottage is marked on Hawley's map (p 29) with his name.

In 1707 Robert Aldred, a priest, came to live in Crosby Hall but there was friction between him and Frances, Nicholas's wife. Seven months later, when Ned Howerd was out of Little Crosby, Nicholas settled the priest in Ned's cottage. On the gable end at the right of the cottage there is a small metal cross marking the attic where mass was secretly celebrated (see below). Nicholas records an occasion when J Kerfrey and Elizabeth Pye came to be married, but as Mr Aldred had gone to Lydiate they stayed until he came after supper and were married then. When Ned returned to the village in April 1713, Nicholas enlarged Mr Aldred's Chapel and added a room to accommodate Ned Howerd. However, these additions were not sufficient and in 1719 Nicholas Blundell began to build a new house and chapel (known as West Lane House) for Mr Aldred opposite to where the present school stands in the village (p 54). It was probably the first Roman Catholic chapel to be built in England since the Reformation.

Mr Robert Aldred

Following the Reformation when Catholics were punished for celebrating the mass Little Crosby remained staunchly Catholic. Mass was secretly celebrated at the Hall both for the family and the villagers and neighbourhood. Even though he was a priest, Rev Robert Aldred SJ (Society of Jesus) was given the title Mr in Nicholas's diary to avoid detection and, for example, it simply says 'Mr Aldred went somewhere abroad'. Besides the cottage and an allowance, Mr Aldred received 'considerable' financial assistance from the yeomen and farmers who were all recusants. For 21 years he was the Diarist's closest friend. On one occasion Nicholas, his wife Frances, and Mrs Blundell of Ince went to Mr Aldred's and 'had a cold supper there brought by both partyes'. Mr Aldred's birthday was celebrated with a bowl of punch and the company of friends. Such diverse subjects as fattening cattle and the celibacy of priests were discussed with him and he helped Nicholas to settle quarrels. When threatened by the authorities he visited Ince and went out coursing to allay suspicion but he would often be forced to hide in the Priest's Hole at Crosby Hall while Frances Blundell hid the vestments and sacred vessels in the 'false roof'. He administered the rite of Holy Oil when Fanny their daughter was desperately ill. More happily, he was involved in the important matter of entertaining their daughter's suitor, providing coffee for the ladies and punch for the men. He died, after a short illness, in 1728.

Smithy and Two Smiths

The last building on the right as you leave the village going to Great Crosby was built in 1713 as the date stone shows (far right). One of the old shoeing blocks can still be seen in front of it by the roadside (right). It is a low, one storey structure, as many of the buildings were originally constructed, to alleviate the effects of the strong winds coming in from the sea. The stones and slates to build the smithy were obtained from Little Crosby Delph (p 30).

The new smithy was built for Richard Webster who had come from nearby Thornton to become village smith. Before that, the post had been held by William Gray. But then Nicholas '*discoursed about changing our Smith William Gray*' and advised him to leave the Town smithy and make one for himself. Why? Then, only the day after William had made some staples for him, Nicholas talked with Richard about '*being Smith in this Town*'. Three weeks later Richard was at work. Whatever William thought of that, he continued to work for Nicholas gaining his gratitude when '*he acquainted me that there was a design against me by Great Crosby, &c: about my Water Courses, he sat with me In the Paintrey [pantry] talking a good while*'. Great secrecy! He was on good terms with Nicholas, supping and drinking with him at the Talbot Inn in Ormskirk after selling a cow for him at the fair.

Richard also did good work for Nicholas, who referred to him as 'our smith' and Nicholas was pleased enough with him to record in October 1719 that he proposed that he continue at the smithy. But Richard owed William money. Two months later, the day after Christmas, William told Nicholas about it and a month after that reported that Richard had run away for debt. On obtaining judgement against Richard, William and Nicholas went to the smithy to gain possession of what was there to pay Mrs Webster's debt. Following that, there was a high level meeting of the overseers of the poor in Little Crosby and Thornton, William Gray, and others to decide responsibility for the maintenance of Mrs Webster and the children. The case went to Liverpool and then Ormskirk for judgement and it was decided that Richard, as a migrant, should be supported by Thornton, his home town. The next smith made sure he paid his rent on time! Later, William was one of the jury appointed by the manor court to see in what state the ditches, paths and fields were in but when Nicholas had to adjust a difference between William and some of his neighbours about an enclosure '*he would not comply with what we all thought reasonable*'. William also had a troublesome daughter: she was too free with her tongue and was 'chastised' for stealing. He left to live in Wexford in 1723.

A Smith's Work

It is not surprising that Smith is the most common English surname when you read in the diaries of Nicholas Blundell how often and in what capacity smiths acted.

Besides shoeing, William Gray was called upon to perform other operations on horses such as docking, bloodying and burning them for lampreys. He 'cleansed' guns that had not been used for a long time (and rusted?) so that Nicholas could immediately go out shooting hawks and larks with the priest. He was asked to make a good warming pan out of two old ones. He bloodied Nicholas the Diarist's workhorses and mended his wife's Dutch table. He also helped Nicholas with odd jobs: taking suckers off the roots of apple trees, pulling up thorns (1,000 of them!), taking the jack to pieces and mending it again (this happened regularly). He advised on the house that Nicholas built for Robert Aldred and doubtless helped build it (p 54).

Richard Webster was similarly employed, installing a new trough in the smithy, fitting up a butler's box with staples for a lock and fixing a new iron stanchion in the brew house window. He also helped Nicholas in other ways by helping him home with coals, finding him a hare set and supplying him with hay.

Wheelwright

Conveniently situated opposite the smithy was a wheelwright. Wooden wheels were fashioned in the shop for traps, wagons and carts. In the 1920s boys used to flock to it and gaze in awe and morbid fascination at the coffins which were made there as well. Two days a week the wheels were bound with metal hoops at the smithy which also supplied fittings for the coffins inside and out. Business was good for the two linked businesses as farming was still prosperous before the recession of the thirties and farmers would get up at 2.30 am to take their produce by road into Liverpool. The wheels and horses' hooves were worn down by the cobbled streets and the smithy would ring with the sound of hammering which attracted the boys with its accompanying smell of burnt hooves and horse droppings. Enterprisingly, George Wharton, the wheelwright, also acted as village undertaker but he was not often called on to do this duty. The Medical Officer of Health often commented on the good health of the village and even in Victorian times someone referred to it as a paradise on earth. Now the building is a brewery ('Rock the Boat') in which the beers are cask conditioned. The inset shows metal bound wood is still there!

Mark Blundell poses with a hoop for a wheel at Crosby Hall

David Barker with a Rock the Boat *barrel of beer*

Shops

Nicholas the Diarist mentions that he spent some time in John Farer's shop. We are not told anything about the contents but apparently it contained enough to interest Nicholas for a while, although much of this may have been spent in conversation. Nicholas and John met frequently on business and social occasions. They often coursed hares together in the mosses and John took care of the harness of Nicholas' horse, mending, lacquering and 'dressing' it. Otherwise Nicholas would shop in Liverpool (maybe going there and back along the shore) or travelling salesmen would call at the Hall.

For centuries the village, as a farming community, was self-sufficient, but by the 1920s the village shop was selling food, drinks, sweets and cigarettes in the front room of a house, and there was another smaller one as well. Milk, poultry and eggs came to houses each side of White House Farm. The rag and bone man with his horse and cart shouted 'Any old iron?' and knives were sharpened on your door step

The depression of the 1930s was followed by war and its aftermath. The village shop closed, and was replaced by a travelling van. A brave attempt was made to revive the shop in the 1960s and 70s but only on conditions set by the Council that it was to be hidden away down the side of Well Farm House, there should be no signs or advertising hoardings telling anyone it was there and no windows were to be put in the part of the house facing the road. It sold produce grown by the Gilbertsons, the owners of the house, and other groceries. The shop closed, succumbing to the attacks of supermarket and retail park, but in 1990 another started in the yard of White House Farm in outbuildings once used as pigsties and stables. A museum was established by Bob Wright in 1996 in farm buildings which flourished for 15 years. It attracted such diverse donations as postcards, medals, toys, church vestments, an 18th century saw and a milking parlour but was disbanded when Bob died in 2011. Now the village is fighting back, with a mini retail park at the Well Barn with beauty salon, florist and kitchen designer.

The village has never had what is often considered marks of a village: a pub, or a post office. However, a 'club' used to be held in the cobbler's shop in Delph Lane where beer was sold at ½d a glass. The room became so crowded and the air so thick that the oil lamps went out. The nearest pub for the Diarist was the Church Inn in Sefton (now the Punch Bowl). The Courtyard Café has filled a gap.

Disturbance of the Peace

On 7th May 1624 bailiffs came to Little Crosby and seized two oxen and a nag belonging to a tenant farmer in Little Crosby, who had failed to pay a sum of £20 he had been fined for being a recusant Catholic. According to one bailiff's account, when they came near the village '*there came…half a hundred persons or thereabouts out of litle Crosby, beinge able people and well weaponed with pykeforks, longstaves, and muchroukes, one speare or pyke for warre and other weapons, severall together in Troupes against them.*' The villagers drove off the bailiffs '*and wounded two of them verie sore… William Blundell and Emilia his wife …incourraged the persons who made the rescue.*' This was not an isolated event. The bailiff later said that when on previous occasions they had been '*going through the towne of Ormskirk unto litle Crosby to make seizure for the Kinge… they were sure not to carrie anything away from thence for hee himself and five or sixe with him had divers tymes gonne into litle Crosby upon like occasions but still they were resisted, beaten or strucken and could bringe nothinge away with them unlesse it was in the night tyme*'. It was said that when the Sheriff's officers came on the scene '*all the young men of Little Crosby have come forth in women's apparell, and have withstoode and made resistance to the Sheriff's officers*'. It is puzzling why they appeared in women's apparel.

There was also the problem of William Stock, a villager, who '*was either a real or counterfeit madman*' who '*struck several people without any manner of cause*' and '*did frequently strip himself almost naked & in the open daylight and run & so continue running as if it were near unto his best speed through the highways and private paths for a mile or two together as if he had been running a race*'. He also frequently walked through the town ringing a bell, and set a field of gorse on fire in several places, as well as burning a stack of turf. Poor crazy Stock was brought before the Court in Ormskirk in 1690 and fined 38s 6d, to be collected by the Constables of Little Crosby.

In the 18th century the destitute might be forced out of the village so that they might not be a burden on the inhabitants (p 40) and it was not uncommon for relatives or friends to harbour poor people to establish residence in order to obtain maintenance. This attitude towards strangers persisted until the early 20th century when a newcomer was 'boycotted'. Allegations were made that his horse had been poisoned by residents and the Squire had to call a special tenants' meeting to resolve the issue.

The contrasting pictures show how it was possible to walk down the street 150 years ago in peace and safety, and for the artist to draw from this viewpoint, but now photographers are in danger of their lives with the disturbance of the traffic.

The picture and photo show three Victorian houses: on the left, dating from 1857; centre middle distance, distinguished by its gable widows, about 1870; on the right, about 1860, behind the tree which has grown! NB the N+B on the front of the house to the left above. Maybe his initials were inserted later or Nicholas Blundell was too modest to include them in his painting! There are still no street lights or electricity or telephone poles.

St Mary's Church

Following the Catholic Emancipation Acts, Catholics were allowed to build places of worship. Consequently, in 1844 William Blundell (p 15) engaged Matthew Ellison Hadfield, one of the leading church architects of the day, to design St Mary's. Built in the early decorated style of Gothic architecture from stone obtained from Little Crosby Delph (p 30), it was consecrated in 1847. The interior decorations were mainly designed and carried out by William's son Nicholas (p 17). He and his sisters lay on their backs on scaffolding and painted the decorative Litany of the Blessed Virgin on the ceiling from stencils they had designed. Unfortunately, though preserved in good condition for over 100 years, the paint eventually crumbled and flaked. In 1977-78 restoration work was

carried out by Mrs Claire Barnes, the Head Teacher of the Village School, who also painted the A and Ω decoration on the Sanctuary Arch. This replaced a depiction of the Last Judgement most probably painted by Nicholas Blundell which unfortunately could not be preserved but can be seen in his painting reproduced opposite.

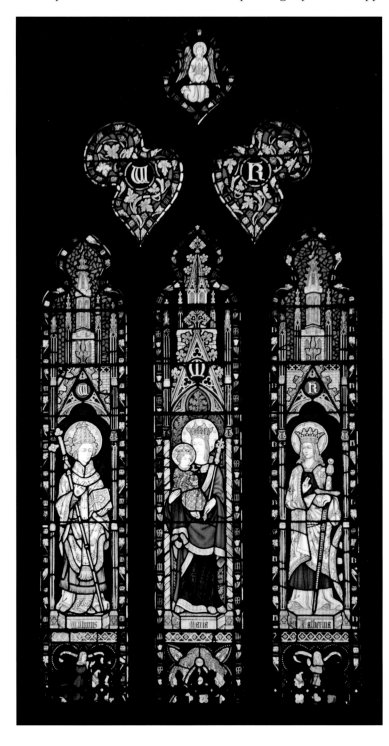

The central figure in the east widow is Mary with Jesus. Her initial M is above her and is balanced by the initials of William and Catherine on either side which also appear in the lunettes above (K is used instead of C). Below these, on either side of Mary, are images of the Saints William and Katherine.

The window seems to have been made in Liverpool to a design by Colonel Nicholas Blundell.

On the left of the Sanctuary are the tomb and effigy of the founder of the Church who died in 1854 (left). On the side of the tomb are the words 'Hic jacet Gulielmus Blundell Armiger Huius Ecclesiae Fundator' (Here lies William Blundell Squire Founder of this Church). The arms of the Blundell of Crosby and Stanley families were carved and painted by his son Colonel Nicholas and Mr Ball. William married Catherine the daughter of Sir Thomas Stanley-Massey-Stanley and she is buried with him.

On the right of the Sanctuary is the Tribune or Private Chapel of the Blundells. In the Tribune is a statue of St Roch who is especially invoked against the plague and is also a patron saint of dogs and falsely accused people, amongst others. It was given by Mary Blundell (see opposite).

Right: St Roch and his dog on the frontispiece of a book in Crosby Hall library (pp 60-61) published in 1808

St Roch

St Roch was born in Montpellier in France in 1295. While attending to people suffering from the plague in the town of Piacenza in Italy, he himself became a victim and was expelled from the town by the authorities. He found shelter in the forest and would have died there had not a dog visited him daily bringing him food. On his recovery, he returned to his native town where he was arrested and imprisoned as a spy. While in prison he died but just before his death he prayed to God that all persons who were stricken with the plague, invoking him, should be made well again.

In the winter of 1889, Little Crosby suffered severely from an epidemic of influenza, during which Colonel Nicholas's wife, Agnes Blundell, and a number of villagers died. Agnes' daughter-in-law, Mary, chose to invoke St Roch. From that time no more deaths occurred and Mary decided to give a statue to the Church depicting him and the dog with a bread roll in its mouth.

Mary was married to Francis Nicholas the 1st, son of Colonel Nicholas Blundell and father of Francis Nicholas the 2nd (p 33). After her husband's early death, she wrote more than fifty books and a number of plays under the pseudonym 'M.E. Francis'. Her first book 'A North Country Village' evokes the life of Little Crosby at the time.

left: Statue of St Roch in the Sanctuary

above: St Roch's dog holding up food for him

Chapel of our Lady and the English Martyrs

The chapel was built in 1885/6 by Colonel Nicholas Blundell as a memorial to his second son, Francis Nicholas, who died in 1884 aged 31. His son, also Francis Nicholas, had the chapel redecorated as a memorial to his father and to his mother Mary who died in 1930. The walls have large paintings with two rows of smaller panels. The row along the top has coats of arms of prominent members of the Blundell family, illustrated here (opposite below) by those of William the Cavalier. Below the main scenes are a series of pictures painted by Francis' friend, Mr, later Mgr, GA Tomlinson, Chaplain to the Roman Catholic students at London University. They depict scenes in the lives of several Roman Catholic martyrs. A particularly interesting one is of St Edmund Arrowsmith as a boy reciting the Little Office of Our Lady, with his companions, on the way to school (right). Edmund, who was martyred in 1628, did not live in Little Crosby, but the artist has imaginatively and symbolically placed the children in the road passing through Little Crosby. Ned Howerd's cottage is in the background in which Mass was said later in the 18th century (pp 38-39).

St Edmund Arrowsmith on his way to school

William the Cavalier (p 11) married Anne, daughter of Sir Thomas Haggerston of Northumberland and his arms impale those of the Haggerstons. Although Little Crosby had a mill (p 20), it was not on a hill and had been removed before the church was built, so the scene is imaginary. The scene on the right with a monastery on a hill and a bridge crossing a river represents Preston and is taken from a contemporary print. William fought with a Royalist force that captured Preston in the early stages of the war but Preston also witnessed Cromwell's victory that ended King Charles's hopes.

Graveyard

Leading up to the church door are the graves of former priests of St Mary's. One not interred here but who served in the church is Father Nugent, a pioneer in 19th century child welfare, poverty relief and social reform in Liverpool. Nugent Care was founded upon his ideals.

Until the 19th century the Blundells were buried in Sefton Church. Then they were buried in St Mary's graveyard at the east end of the church. Among the many graves may be found those of the Squires since the church was built. The following have been mentioned in the book:

(Colonel) Nicholas died 1894 aged 83 and Agnes 1890 aged 65 (pp 16 & 17)
William Joseph died 1909 aged 58 (p 17)
Francis Nicholas [the 2nd] died 1936 aged 56 (p 32) and his wife Theresa died
 1979 aged 87
Also, Francis Nicholas [the 1st] died 1884 aged 31 and his wife Mary died 1930
 aged 71 (p 49)

William Blundell 'Fundator' has his tomb inside the church (pp 15 & 48)

The Graveyard and Presbytery, formerly West Lane House (pp 54-55). The Blundell graves are round the corner on the right.

The Black Death

1349 was the first year of the Black Death, the terrible plague that swept across Europe, wiping out between a third and a half of the population of England. Very few households were entirely spared. We have no details of how it affected Little Crosby or the surrounding manors, but there is ample evidence that Lancashire was as hard hit as any other area of the country. It seems likely that the plague was responsible for a plethora of deaths in the Blundell and Molyneux families. For some the cloud of the Black Death could have a silver lining and John Blundell may have found it. When he was born in about 1330, the manor of Little Crosby had descended from Uctred to the Molyneux family (p 27). There it would have stayed had not a series of deaths occurred, starting in 1349. In that year John Blundell's elder brother died and Richard, the son and heir of Sir John Molyneux, who held the manor of Little Crosby at the time, died in the following year. Although he was married, he left no surviving children and it could be that they were victims of the Black Death too. So John Blundell eventually inherited Little Crosby (p 21).

A May procession passes the church in about 1900

West Lane House

Beyond the Church was the Chapel and the house which Nicholas Blundell the 'Diarist' built for Mr Aldred the priest in 1719 when he moved from Ned Howerd's Cottage (p 38). At this time Roman Catholics still had to worship in secret, and in the deeds concerning this Chapel it is always called 'West Lane House' and the priest was always referred to as 'Mr'; the tenant was never a 'priest' (p 39).

Right: date stone at rear of West Lane house.

Excitement during the building of the House

Nicholas Blundell the Diarist drew up the plans or drawings for it himself and more or less supervised the building operations after taking advice from the smith William Gray (pp 40-41). While it was in the course of erection, customs men came along on 27th April 1720 and searched the building for smuggled brandy. Some of the local gentry, Nicholas Blundell among them, did engage now and again in smuggling wines and spirits from France, and indeed shortly after this search Charles Howerd, the village tailor, Nicholas, and Robert Aldred were dealing in bottling large quantities of claret and brandy and selling them to the gentlemen of the district. One day Nicholas mixed eight gallons of French brandy and on another received eleven gallons of claret. Mr Thomas, the customs officer, was helped in his search by Thomas Marrow, the village constable (also the village tailor, p 36). They went through the outhouses of the Hall and the partly built West Lane House. Evidently they must have failed in their search but what excitement it must have provided the men engaged on the building!

With the remission of restrictions on Roman Catholic worship, West Lane House was substantially extended in 1782 (date stone below) and recognised as a place of public worship. When St Mary's Church was built, it was altered in 1858 to be used as a Presbytery, Convent and School. The west extension was face-lifted with a shield showing the Blundell arms and the arms of Catherine Stanley, wife of William Blundell Fundator (see picture opposite and photo on page 52). On the south side of the School are still to be seen the windows of the 1782 Chapel, but these are not visible from the road. The School was replaced by a modern building across the road in 1963 but West Lane House continued as a Presbytery and Convent for some years. They are now used as private houses.

NᵻB: *Nicholas ✝ Blundell*

St Mary's Church and West Lane House in the 1860s

Blundell shield on West Lane House

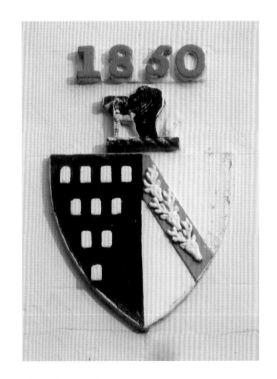

Shield with the arms of Catherine Stanley, wife of William 'Fundator'

Crosby Hall

If you turn right at the Church into Back Lane (400 yards on the right), you will arrive at the entrance to Crosby Hall. As Hawley's map shows (p 20) this road then led no further than the Hall. The main road (no longer existing) ran off to the left.

Crosby Hall is the family home of the Blundells of Crosby, the lords of the manor, the place associated with the family for over 750 years. The earliest mention of a Hall at Little Crosby is in a document dated 1275, and even then it is referred to as the 'Old Hall'. This, of course, has long since disappeared. The present Hall is thought to date from about 1609, though there is a stone dated 1576 on it (see below). An old drawing of the Hall (opposite) shows a smaller building standing beside the 1609 building, together with a large gate house. This might have been an old manor house of Tudor design. This and the gate house were pulled down when some extensive alterations and additions were made to the 1609 building in 1784-6. Various later wings were added to the structure to give it a somewhat rambling appearance (opposite below), but some demolition and alterations carried out in 1953-5 have brought the building back again to the dignified symmetrical structure it was in 1609 (above).

Above: View from north west showing the greatly enlarged Hall

*Left: Inserted on front of Hall: **R**ichard **B**lundell (died 1592), **A**nne **B** his wife and **W**illiam **B** his son (p 9)*

Crosby Hall 1736.

Crosby Hall Grounds

During the course of changes in the 18th century, the forecourt and formal gardens of the house were swept away (the sundial in the garden is dated 1768). John Webb surveyed and landscaped the park in 1815, with shelter belt tree planting, ha-has and an impressive rock arch called the 'Dragon's Teeth'.

Left: the 'Dragon's Teeth'

Right: the formal gardens at the rear of the Hall in the 1880s

Below: cows chewing the cud in the park

Right below: a performance for children in front of the rotunda

Crosby Hall Library

William 'Fundator' (p 15) created the library in about 1815 and in his lifetime (to 1854) built up a collection of over 3,000 volumes. Consequently, most of them date from the 17th to mid 19th century. The architect is not recorded but could be John Webb of Staffordshire who surveyed and landscaped the park in 1815, and was a protégé of Wyatt who was active in Lancashire, for example Liverpool Town Hall. The bookcases are of mahogany with ebony inlay surmounted by busts (below, of Homer and Aphrodite). The others are Cicero, Demosthenes (reflected in mirror opposite), Octavian (left opposite) and Aeschines (right opposite). There is a contemporary bronze chandelier (right) perhaps by George Bullock of Liverpool. The collection is particularly strong in the Classics, History, Literature, Religion and Travel. Art and Architecture, Biography and Memoirs, Geography and Journals are also well represented and there are a significant number of books on Natural History, Philosophy and Education but little on Science or Medicine.

The oldest book in the library (title page below) contains the writings of the ancient Greek orator Isocrates (436-338 BC), published in 1570. Appropriately, he died at the great age of 98.

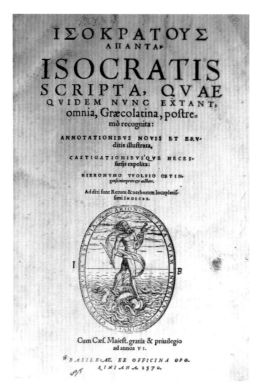

Left: one of the two doors disguised with false book backs. This leads from the main entrance hall. Another one led into the ballroom which has been demolished and the doorway blocked up (to the right above).

Crosby Hall Educational Trust (CHET) and the Great Barn

To the north of the Hall are the early 17th century stables and the Great Barn which may be 16th or even 15th century, and is the oldest part of the Hall and outbuildings still standing. It is a stout building with huge oak beams supporting the roof. This is the barn where for centuries the customary festivities of the Township were held right down to the early part of the 20th century. In 1988 the old farm and stables of Crosby Hall were converted into accommodation to run residential courses for schoolchildren. Crosby Hall Educational Trust or CHET, as it became known, was founded by Mark Blundell and his wife Suzanne and opened by Princess Margaret in 1991. It co-operates with local schools, as well as wider partners, to run indoor and outdoor activities and also concerts

and other annual programmes. CHET is now the means by which the traditions and special character of Crosby Hall are being harnessed to serve the modern ecumenical world.

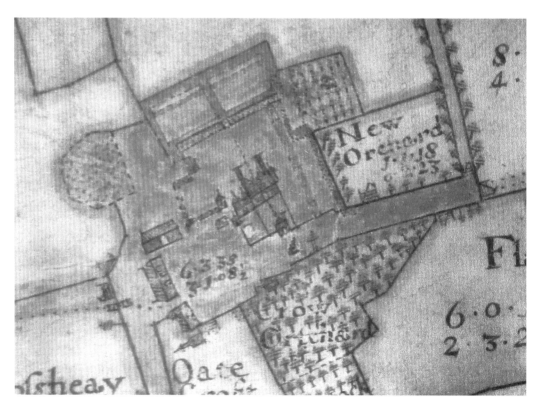

Above right: the Great Barn as part of CHET is far left.

Below: the Great Barn is centre left on Hawley's map of 1702. Compare the plan of the house (centre) with the picture on the top of page 57.

Above: Squire Francis Blundell (p 33) talks pig production with his manager in the farmyard which is now part of CHET.

Below: the Great Barn is centre overlooking a social occasion.

Harkirk

Catholic recusants were not automatically entitled to burial in the consecrated ground of the parish churchyard at Sefton and the Rectors had the right to refuse such burials. In 1610 William Blundell the Recusant (pp 9 & 66) *'caused a little peece of grownde to bee enclosed within my owne demaine land in a place called of ould tyme (as it is nowe also) the Harkirke.'* This was to become the burying ground. The Harkirk site was a place of religious significance in pre-Conquest times and 'Harkirk' means old (or grey) church in Anglo-Saxon. Although the site of the Harkirk is now well concealed inside the park at Crosby Hall, at the time a road from Crosby Hall to Sefton ran very near it, as Hawley's

map of 1702 shows. There is still in existence a small book, the Harkirk Burial Register, in which were written the names of all the people buried there. In all 131 names are recorded over a period of 142 years. Until May 1629, the great majority of the 104 buried were lay people – only five were priests. On the orders of the Star Chamber the Harkirk burial ground was destroyed, probably sometime in 1629. William's daughter Margaret, now Sister Winifred, recorded the event though she cannot actually have witnessed it as she was in an enclosed convent in France. She says *'…when about eighty had been buried there, comes the High Sheriff with thirty men and pulled down the walls, knocking the stones to pieces, both those on the wall and those that lay upon the graves, and carried away the crosses in mocking manner, also digging some part of the graves; and sounded their trumpet coming away in great pomp'.* The work was done thoroughly, and only one gravestone survived which is incorporated in a wall of the memorial chapel (left) built on the Harkirk site in 1889 by Colonel Nicholas Blundell.

Opposite below: a group of stones built into the wall of the chapel. On the left is the gravestone of John Layton (I. LA.) a priest (P) of the Society of Jesus (SO.IES) buried in 1624. In the centre is a memorial stone to 'Mr Rob(er)t Aldred Feb(ruar)y 3 1727/8' (the day he died, pp 38-39). On the right of the display is an inscription starting with IHS, the Latin letter form of the Greek initial letters for 'Jesus, Son of God, Saviour' with a cross over the H.

Above: William Blundell's account of how he established the Harkirk Burial Ground in December 1610.

Harkirk Hoard

On 8th April 1611, the day after the first burial in the graveyard, William Blundell the Recusant (pp 9 & 64) recorded that a servant boy named Thomas, '*dryvinge my Catle (which as yett did nightlie lye in the howse) to a field neare the sayde place of buriall*', found some ancient coins which had been buried but were disturbed by the digging. On investigation, further coins were found, to a total of about 80. A churchyard is a likely place to hide a hoard of treasure and probably they had belonged to an Anglo-Saxon or Dane, burying the coins before fleeing in a time of trouble. William and his household had never seen anything like them, '*none bigger than a groate, and none less than a twoe pence.*' William set to work to delve into the origins of the coins, with the help of books in his library. His reading was wide and he was unusually well acquainted with some of the major authors of the past. The hoard turned out to include coinage of the Saxon kings Alfred the Great and Edward the Elder, and the Danish king Cnut of Northumbria. William carefully copied thirty-five of them in pen and ink (see right), and had an engraving made on a copper plate. Prints were made from this, eventually up to 200, which '*flew abroad in ye country*'. These coins he kept in his possession, though they were subsequently lost during the Civil War when William the Cavalier sent them with other valuables to his relations in Wrexham, ironically '*for better security in ye tyme of war*'. The remainder were melted down and turned into a chalice and a pyx. Sadly the chalice has since disappeared but the pyx (a small container for communion hosts) survives to this day. It is now in the British Museum (opposite below, obverse and reverse). The coins fascinated William, and he devoted a lengthy essay to them upon which his reputation as an 'Antiquary' is based. Nationally, the Harkirk hoard was the first discovery of buried coins of the Anglo-Saxon period and was therefore, and has remained, of the greatest interest to antiquarians and numismatists. Though more accurate professional identifications were made later, in many cases William's assessments of the coins were not far out.

Below: Another Blundell treasure in the British Museum is this rare pre-reformation rosary with detail of a bead.

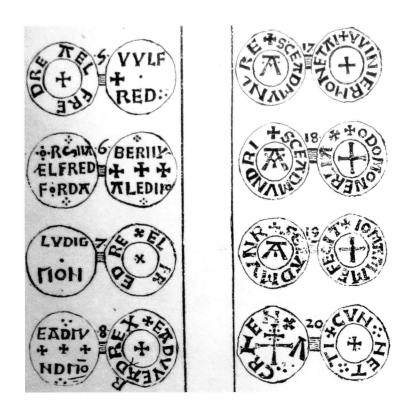

'This was made of silver found in the burial place W.B.'

Sunnyfields Cottage

Passing the entrance to Crosby Hall and CHET as you go down Back Lane, you come to a right angle turn to the left in the road and then the road turns right. Straight on was (and is) the path used for many generations by the Blundells of Crosby to visit their namesakes at Ince. Sunnyfield Path was created by Nicholas Blundell (1741-1795) and his friend Henry Blundell of Ince (the great collector of antiquities, see caption opposite) expressly for the exclusive use of the two families. If you wish to follow their journey, there is a beautiful walk across the fields and through the woods to the A565 but the entrance to Ince Park on the other side has been bricked up. In the wood there is a deep ditch marking the boundary between the two estates after the dispute of 1437 (see opposite) known to this day as the Division Ditch.

The gardener's cottage (below) on the corner is now known as Sunnyfields Cottage. It was designed for Colonel Nicholas Blundell by T Mellard Reade who also laid out the Blundellsands estate for him in 1868. As well as an architect and civil engineer, Reade was also a noted geologist who debated the age of the earth in the Darwin evolution controversy.

A great grandfather of George Harrison (the Beatle) was head gardener at Crosby Hall and lived in the cottage. When he died in 1890 George's grandmother, aged ten, had to move from the cottage as it came with the job.

The Blundells of Crosby and Ince

The Crosby Blundells must not be confused with the Blundells of Ince who used to reside at Ince Blundell Hall, a mile away. Blundell is a Norman name (it means 'fair-haired' in Norman-French) and was adopted by Robert Blundell of Crosby in the early 13th century. There could have been a connection with the Ince family at that time. Alice, daughter of Nicholas Blundell of Crosby (c1360-1422), married William Blundell of Ince, but this was the only intermarriage between the two neighbouring families. In 1437 Nicholas' son Henry was involved in a dispute with his brother-in-law William Blundell of Ince over the boundary between the two manors. In the 19th century the Ince Blundell estate passed to the Weld family, one of whom adopted the name Weld-Blundell and came to live at Ince. His descendants ceased to live at Ince after the 1950s and since 1960 the house has been run as a nursing home by the Canonesses of St Augustine of the Mercy of Jesus.

Ince Blundell Hall in the early 20th century. On the right is an extension modelled on the Pantheon in Rome. From the 1760s onwards Henry Blundell collected ancient sculptures, and he built this and a temple in the gardens to house them. A few of them are now on display in the Walker Art Gallery, Liverpool.

It was through this lodge that the Blundells would make their way to Sefton and Ormskirk. There is a track across the fields in the park from the Hall leading to the lodge, still quite visible and used by farmers. Within memory, the mother of the family would open the gate on hearing the sound of the approaching coach's horn! The coach would then pass the Bailiff's House (pp 15 & 23) which still survives as a farm house in Virgin's Lane.

Right: Sefton Church in Victorian times depicted by John Harwood, born 13 July 1798, as imagined on his future unfinished gravestone.

St Helen's Church at Sefton

St Helen's Church at Sefton, three miles away, is the oldest in the area and the only grade I listed building in the Borough of Sefton to which it gave its name. Its buildings date from the 15th and 16th centuries but the tower and spire are from the 1300s and there are stone fragments indicating a small chapel of the 12th century. After the Reformation it became an Anglican Church and was the parish church for the whole area until 1853 when the daughter parish of St Luke's, Great Crosby, was formed. Others followed so that it is now the mother and grandmother of 29 local churches. On one side of the church is the 'Blundell Chapel' where members of the family were buried. Little Crosby residents were expected to attend the church when their allegiance to the Church of England and the Crown was being tested. Even after the Reformation when Crosby Hall and Little Crosby still held to their Catholic faith and were persecuted for it, the Blundells sometimes kept up a good relationship with the church and its rectors. Nicholas Blundell, the Diarist, acted as Churchwarden, was friendly with the Parson and records many convivial visits to the Parsonage and the adjacent Church Inn, now the Punch Bowl.

Below: left: the original gravestone in Sefton Church of Nicholas the Diarist and his daughter; right: an additional inscription on the family grave shows how the line continued through the marriage of Frances with Henry Pippard (pp 13 & 72).

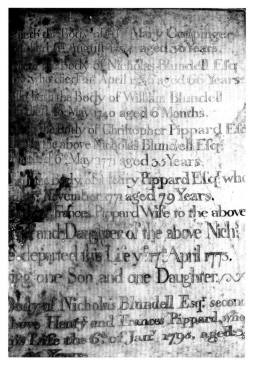

Here Lieth the body of Nicholas Blundell of Little Crosby Esqr who departed this Life the 21st of April 1737 aged 68 Also the body of Mary Coppinger his daughter who departed this life the 6th August 1734 aged 30th May they rest in Peace

Nicholas died in 1737, not 1736

The Blundells of Little Crosby (Lords of the Manor are in **bold**)

Relationship to preceding: s = son, d = daughter, b = brother, sis = sister

Osbert of Ainsdale (?-1160) m. ? Held Manor of Ainsdale p 6

s. **Robert of Ainsdale** (?-1214) m. ? Held Manor of Great Crosby p 6

s. **Adam** (?-1260) m. Emma (of Ince?)

s. **Sir Robert Blundell** (c.1210-1278) m. Maud of Montgomery Took name Blundell p 6

s. **Nicholas^{I}** (c.1235-1321) m. Eleanor

s. **David** (c.1255-1311) m. Agnes Molyneux Dau. of Sir John Molyneux pp 6, 27

s. **Nicholas^{II}** (c.1295-1349) m. Aline of Holland

s. **John** (c.1330-1374) m. Emma ~ First Blundell Lord of Manor of Little Crosby p 21

b. **Henry^{I}** (c.1335-1405) m. Ellen Page

s. **Nicholas^{III}** (c.1360-1422) m. Ellen Tyldesley Knight of the Shire p 69

s. **Henry^{II}** (c.1385-1457) m.Joan Rixton

s. **Nicholas^{IV}** (d.c.1476) m.~ Salmesbury

s. **Nicholas^{V}** (c.1443-1523) m.Margaret Scarisbrick Molyneux Quarrel p 27

s. **Henry^{III}** (c.1465-1513) m.(1) Katherine Heaton Killed at Flodden 1513 p 27

s. **James** (1491-1527) m. Margaret Butler

s. **Henry^{IV}** (1517-1556) m. Anne Leyland

s. **Richard** (1537-1592) m. Anne Starkie Died in prison p 9

s. **William^{I}** (1560-1638) m. Emilia Norris 'the Recusant' p 9

s. Nicholas^{VI} (c.1590-1631) m. Jane Bradshaigh

s. **William^{II}** (1620-1698) m. Anne Haggerston 'the Cavalier' p 11

s. Nicholas^{VII} (1640-1680) Priest

b. **William^{III}** (1645-1702) m. Mary Eyre (1643-1707)

s. **Nicholas^{VIII}** (1669-1737) m. Frances Langdale 'the Diarist' p13

d. Mary (1704-1734) m. John Coppinger p 13

sis. **Frances** (1706-1773) m. Henry Pippard (d.1771) p 13

s. **Nicholas^{IX}** (1741-1795) m. Clementina Tempest Took name Blundell p 68

s. **William Joseph^{I}** (1786-1854) m. Catherine Stanley-Massey-Stanley 'Fundator' p 15

s. **Nicholas^{X}** (1811-1894) m. Agnes Smythe 'the Colonel' p 17

s. **William Joseph^{II}** (1851-1909) m. Cecily de Trafford p 17

b. Francis Nicholas^{I} (1853-1884) m. Mary Sweetman 'Tansy' p 49

s. **Francis Nicholas^{II}** (1880-1936) m. Theresa Ward p 33

s. **Nicholas^{XI}** (1925-1949)

sis. **Hester** (1928-2000) m. Brian Whitlock p 17

s. **Mark** (1950-) m. Suzanne Glatz pp 42 & 62